OLDHAM
in old photographs
by
Eric Krieger

Front cover: *Oldham, Yorkshire Street.*

Published by Hendon Publishing Co. Ltd., Hendon Mill, Nelson, Lancashire.
Text © Eric Krieger 1988
Printed by Fretwell & Cox Ltd., Goulbourne Street, Keighley, West Yorkshire BD21 1PZ.

Introduction

'Such places as had become rather large villages by the prosperity of the domestic spinning and weaving concerns, were transformed by the factory system into great and increasing towns.' These comments of Edwin Butterworth appeared in his *Historical Sketches of Oldham* (1856); the town then had a population in excess of 50,000 and was expanding yearly.

Oldham is nothing if not a product of the nineteenth century. By 1800 the ancient woollen trade was almost extinct, and although there had been a revival of a traditional hatting industry, and coal mines, the people numbered a modest 10–12,000. A century later Oldham's textile mills were counted in their hundreds. The town had won both Parliamentary representation and a municipal charter, was connected to the national rail networks, displayed dignified Victorian architecture and was home to more than 100,000 souls.

According to Douglas Farnie in *The Cotton Mills of Oldham* (1985), by 1866 the town's mills held more spindles than any other centre in the world, and five years later, more than any country other than the USA. Oldham not only spun its yarns, but firms such as Platt Bros. and Asa Lees engineered the machinery to do so, also equipping other factories at home and abroad. To quote Mr Farnie, 'Platt's mules were the true basis of the industrial supremacy of Oldham.'

It was no small advantage to the town's mechanised factories that Oldham sat on workable coal seams. Butterworth claims that in 1825 the township mined thirty collieries; a hundred years on, Kelly's Directory was still asserting that 'coal mines furnish a large share of the local trade'.

'Roughyeds', that popular soubriquet for Oldhamers, is said to owe its origin to the coarse felt hats produced here, 24 factories turning out 12,000 a week in 1822. Thomas Henshaw's Bluecoat School remains as a tangible memorial to one of Oldham's leading headwear manufacturers.

Until 1849 Oldham was governed by an unelected body known as the Police Commissioners. That year the Charter of Incorporation provided for an elected Council, but not before the Commissioners had put up a Town Hall in 1841. In 1853, the local authority acquired gas and water supplies, previously in private ownership. It did not act as a transport undertaking until 1900, when the first electric trams ran; prior to this the Council had laid down tracks for lease to other enterprises operating horse and steam traction.

Elementary education was administered by the School Board — a directly elected body — from 1871 to 1903; from 1 January 1904, powers were transferred to the Council's Education Committee.

One of the Corporation's most ambitious schemes was the laying out of Alexandra Park. Opened in 1865, this project gave work to textile operatives unemployed due to the cotton famine caused by the American Civil War.

The 1832 Reform Act enabled towns such as Oldham to petition for representation at Westminster. William Cobbett and John Fielden were voted Oldham's first M.P.s.

Attempts to link Oldham to Manchester by rail were considered in the 1820s, but it was not until 1842 that Werneth Station was opened. By the turn of the century there were stations at Hollinwood, Werneth, Clegg Street (Central), Mumps and Royton Junction (all Lancashire & Yorkshire); Clegg Street and Glodwick Road (Oldham, Ashton & Guide Bridge).

Union Street was Oldham's proudest thoroughfare. As the nineteenth century matured, architectural aesthetes could admire the Lyceum (Italianate, 1856), Library ('vague Gothic', 1883) and public baths (1854, altered 1880). Fun-seekers had to await the new century for the Grand Theatre (1908), Palace (1908), Palladium (1913) and Grosvenor (1920).

Sporting parochials could watch cricket in the Central Lancashire League from 1892, although League soccer was not contested until 1907 when the Latics gained entry to Division II.

Edwardian Oldham inherited from its Victorian yesterday a town of smokestack skylines and terraced houses, trams and trains, cotton mills and brass bands, theatre and learning, escapist fantasy and grim reality. Much of this life was reflected for those erstwhile Oldhamers in that humble but pervasive creation, the pictorial postcard. Indeed, it would be no great exaggeration to suggest that before the Great War there were picture postcards of everything: bishop and actress, stage and sport, transport and tragedy, high art and low life, markets and mayhem, roads and royalty.

Britain's first postcards were produced in 1870, but these were plain prepaid official issues. By 1894 the Post Office permitted the affixing of adhesive stamps, giving scope for private publishers to print their own cards with pictorial designs. Not until 1899 were the familiar (5½" × 3½") standard sized postcards allowed, and in 1902 a line dividing one side into message and address halves was sanctioned, enabling the illustration to appear 'full out' on the other.

In 1905 Oldham had up to nine postal collections a day with two on Sunday; a letter reaching the main office by 11 a.m. would be delivered to Saddleworth before 2 p.m. and centrally within the hour. Small wonder that postcards served as surrogate telephones, with a message timed 10 a.m. advising of a visitation at 4 p.m. the same day.

They were not only used to convey brief forewarnings and cryptic intelligencies, but many were purchased for collection and preservation in decorated, embossed albums. Enthusiasts boasted of their latest acquisitions, exchanged cards and perused hobbyists' journals.

In order to satisfy this voracious market, producers emerged everywhere, ranging in size from the giant fine art printers with their legions of engravers, photographers and salesmen, to the one man back-street jobbing cameramen.

Valentine of Dundee and Raphael Tuck of London saw Oldham's photographic prospects in large public buildings, busy highways and Alexandra Park. Local photographers focused their lenses on the idiosyncratic shots of the ephemeral: Whit Walks, railway smash, sporting event, Wakes fun-fair, or perhaps Oldham children posed in quiet cobbled streets. Stationers and booksellers commissioned cards under their own imprint, but from whatever source these rectangular souvenirs have provided an invaluable window on to the town of yesteryear.

Many of the photographs in this volume are taken from some of these early picture postcards, and perhaps the true creators of the book are photographic artists such as William McQueen of Royton, Harry Wheatley of Beechey Street, George Rowland of King Street and other uncredited and unidentified craftsmen who composed and captured these fascinating images of bygone Oldham.

Yorkshire Street. An artistic and gentrified mid-nineteenth-century impression of Oldham's Town Hall area. The original work has been photographed for a cabinet print, with typical late Victorian gilded lettering to the reverse of the mounting board identifying the copier as William Diggle ('Portrait & Landscape Photographer') of Westwood House, 154, Middleton Road.

Family Group.   Cabinet photograph by Partington of Featherstall Road.

Cabinet Photograph.   There can have been few late Victorian households without its cabinet photographs, either framed or slotted into purposely designed albums. The mounting board usually advertised the photographer and his studio; this spruce young man's vignette was the creation of Dyson of King Street. His studio was later the workplace of George Rowland who photographed Oldham and its twentieth-century townspeople.

Oldham Town Hall. Before Oldham was granted its 1849 Charter of Incorporation, the townsfolk were governed by a non-elective body known as the Police Commissioners. Established under an Act of 1826, their qualification for office was based on property; either paying £30 per year in rent or receiving £50 per annum, entitled them to administer services such as highway maintenance, street lighting, sanitary needs, fire brigade and police. They were empowered to levy a tax, but within limits. The Act made provision for the Commissioners to *'erect and build or otherwise to provide and maintain a town hall or public building with fit and convenient public offices therein for holding meetings and transacting . . . business . . . and to provide watch houses and lock up houses . . . wherein may be lodged any night walkers, felons, malefactors, vagrants, beggars, and disturbers of the peace . . .'* The first stone of Oldham's Town Hall was laid in April 1840, and by August the following year, the people were able to admire their new 'tetrastyle Ionic portico'. The site had cost £1,700, the building £4,810, and a further £25 was expended on a pair of lamps.

The days of the Commissioners were numbered. A Municipal Corporation Act in 1835 allowed for ratepayers of charterless towns to petition Parliament for a more representative form of self-government. A period of unrest in Oldham had seen magistrates bring in rural police to quell riots, and this intrusion led to demands in some quarters for a town charter. Oldham's Charter of Incorporation (13 June 1849) arrived in the town the following morning; it was encased in a tin box (cost: 2*s.* 9*d.*).

The desire for a charter had not been universal — some believed this would be more costly than without — and there was no small irony in the result of the inaugural council election. The anti-incorporators took the most votes in that historic poll, conducted on 2 August. Oldham's first mayor was William Jones, the son of a Welsh mine owner, who had himself come to Oldham as a labourer early in the nineteenth century. Mr Jones represented Werneth, one of the eight wards into which the town had been partitioned; the others were: St James's, Waterhead Mill, Clarksfield, Mumps, St Peter's, St Mary's and Westwood.

Mayor of Oldham's 'Lamb' Holiday Fund, 1933. The caption to this postcard nearly says it all. The fund was to enable children, in their last year at school and who had never been to the seaside, to make a visit to the coast. In July 1933, they were off to Hoylake.

The origin of the fund's name was said to derive from the gift of a young lamb, offered by a Welsh farmer to a local councillor, J.T. Petty, who found the woolly beast something of a problem. What to do with it? He presented the animal to a former mayor, Isaac Crabtree, who found a home for it in one of the town's hospitals. The four-footed inspiration then acted as a symbol of the fund, to which donations were given for the Oldham children's seaside outings.

George V and Queen Mary at Platt's Works, July 1913. The 1913 royal tour of the County Palatine began on Monday 7 July, with a rail journey to Warrington from London, and ended the following Monday after a State visit to Manchester. They had come to see the industries of Lancashire and *'the men and women on whose devotion and energies, under Providence, those industries depend.'* An estimated 90 per cent of the county's population cast welcoming eyes on the royal guests. Over 200 of the 250 processional miles were taken by chauffeured motor car.

On 12 July, at 11.15 a.m., they entered the town via Hathershaw, after paying their respects to Ashton-under-Lyne. The elements — responsive to neither wishes, nor wills — threatened rain, delivered a shower or two, but cleared to give sunshine when most needed. The streets, garlanded and Union Jacked, betokened warmth and welcome, even if one ungenerous commentator proffered the opinion that the *'decoration appeared less as an adornment than to take the eye away from buildings which no stretch of the imagination could regard as imposing.'*

At Hathershaw a floral arch spanned the road; 'Welcome to Oldham' its message and the Boys' Life Brigade Band struck up the National Anthem. At Copster Hill and Lee Street tramway standards carried salutations — 'Hearty Greetings' and 'Long Live Our King and Queen'. Along Union Street 1,500 pensioners waited outside the Reform Club, and on to Rhodes Bank where the crowds had been gathering since 6.30 a.m. At Horsedge Street Ireland's Oldhamers hung their own felicitations: 'Caed mille failthe' (a thousand welcomes).

A carpeted and canopied platform by the Town Hall enabled the monarch to raise his brown bowler hat in response to the clamorous welcome. Introductions to the mayor, Alderman Ashworth, and other local worthies completed, the first townsman called for three cheers, and then the King ('looking bronzed and well') took his seat once more in the leading car, as the convoy made for Werneth Park.

Here Oldham's 14,000 elementary scholars, with their teachers, cheered the royal tourists before the party made for the mighty textile machinery workshop of Platt's, where they were frozen for our photograph.

Lees Road Primitive Methodists, Whit Friday 1907. 'Oldham donned holiday dress this (Friday) morning. Mills were stopped, workshops shut; some new flags were flying from public buildings and private premises and many were waving in the breeze above Sunday school processions; people were — in the early hours — making their way to the railway stations, and later others thronged the footpaths, interested spectators of the children marching past; vehicular traffic was suspended; the centre of the borough had on a busy air, but it was not the ordinary work-a-day briskness, for everyone was on holiday . . . The chief ornament of the town this morning was the long ranks of happy looking children . . . making their way to their Sunday Schools . . . before setting out on the annual parade.' *Oldham Evening Chronicle,* Friday, 24 May 1907.

Oldham War Memorial. Unveiled by General Sir Ian Hamilton on 28 April 1923, the ceremony was witnessed by an estimated gathering of 10,000. One intrepid onlooker surveyed the proceedings from the roof of the Greaves Arms. The sculptor, Albert Toft, and site architect, Tom Taylor, saw the fruits of their labours formally accepted by the mayor, Councillor Freeman, from the War Memorial Committee and subscribers. The dedication was given by the Bishop of Manchester, Dr Temple.

Oldham Royal Infirmary, Union Street West. The earliest parts of the infirmary date from 1872, although benefactions have enabled several subsequent enlargements. A Nicholls Ward was added in 1877 and the gift from a William Richardson provided for another ward in 1881. The laundry and dispensary of 1883 were built through a bequest of Asa Lees. Queen Victoria's reign was commemorated in the shape of a new wing, giving forty-four extra beds.

As if all this generosity was not enough, the proceeds from the Grosvenor cinema's opening day afternoon screening in August 1920 were donated to the hospital; one of the films on show was aptly referred to as a 'healthy comedy'.

Westhulme Hospital, Christmas c. 1910. Until 1877 Oldham had no accommodation for those unfortunates suffering from infectious diseases. An increase in the number of smallpox cases, however, caused the Council to apply its collective mind to the problem, deciding to erect a temporary hospital at Westhulme.

The fears of a doubtful public were allayed by permitting inspection during the week prior to opening; an estimated 13,000 visitors had their anxieties thus lessened. In order to overcome the reluctance of mothers to part with sick children, they were permitted, in 1880, to join their offspring in hospital.

A new wing in 1882 relieved some overcrowding, but following an 1887 scarlet fever epidemic in the town, it was decided to build a permanent brick structure. With the introduction of the Strinesdale Isolation Hospital, Westhulme ceased to take smallpox cases in 1894. Four years later the extended hospital stood in seven acres of grounds. A sanatorium block, which was opened in 1914 to treat tuberculosis patients, was destroyed in 1940.

In the early years the institution was hardly overstaffed! It employed a matron (£35 per annum), two female nurses (£20 per annum), one probationary nurse (£14 per annum) and a man and wife for general duties (£50 per annum).

High Street, F.W. Woolworth.   In October 1983, Oldham Council granted permission for the demolition of the town's Woolworth building, and the following January, one of High Street's most familiar shopping venues closed its doors for the last time.

The Oldham store opened in 1925 and was later enlarged. The American Frank Winfield Woolworth's first British venture was at Liverpool; other towns and cities then adopted these low-price bazaars. Oldhamers entering this branch were reminded (as if that was necessary) on the long sign above the doors, that they were at the '3*d* and 6*d* store'.

The passing electric tram is on the 20 route to Waterhead.

High Street, looking westwards. In a sketch map, labelled *Oldham As It Appeared About 1756,* this ancient thoroughfare is identified as 'Main Street'. It connected the then road to Manchester, Water Street, in one direction, with the route to Saddleworth and Ashton, Church Street and Bow Street, in the other. This map, reproduced as an inset to a contemporary nineteenth-century plan of Oldham published in James Butterworth's 1817 history, contrasts the modest eighteenth-century village with the embryonic town. In the later chart, Main Street had become High Street and several other familiar byways had acquired their modern designations, including Union Street and the lower end of Yorkshire Street which were still undeveloped.

Even though a Manchester-Austerlands Turnpike Trust was authorised by an Act of 1734, Oldham was not adequately linked to Manchester and Yorkshire until later in the century, when Manchester Street was constructed and town centre improvements made. By 1790 Oldham was a stopping-point for Manchester-Wakefield stage-coaches.

Within 30 years Butterworth was complaining that *'High Street, in which at present is carried on the chief traffic, is in some parts very narrow, so as scarcely to admit two carriages to pass, particularly that part which connects with Yorkshire Street, the narrowness of which is disgraceful to the town itself.'*

Market Place. This photograph of Market Place is scarcely recognizable to the modern eye. As an aid to orientation, the building to the right of the tram, the Old Cheshire Cheese public house, stands at the corner of Henshaw Street on the site later occupied by C & A's store. To the left of the lamp is the top of George Street.

According to Hartley Bateson's history, a Saturday street market probably existed in the town centre before 1790, although this venue at Old Market Place did not become established until 1804.

The combined ornamental lamp and drinking fountain was provided by the King Street Co-operative Society as a commemoration of Queen Victoria's Golden Jubilee. It cost £250 and was unveiled by the society's president on 21 January 1888. The festivity was dampened by the weather, the '. . . speakers [being] under the necessity of addressing their remarks to a conspicuous crowd of umbrellas'. The same organisation had donated an earlier fountain, and again on the day of the grand occasion, 9 April 1859, 'the rain came down in torrents'. Both of these gifts later found themselves re-erected in the park square; the structure featured in this view was removed from the park area in the early 1950s.

The electric tram is awaiting its descent to Manchester.

Market Hall from Albion Street. Markets have long been newsworthy. The first edition of the *Oldham Chronicle,* dated 6 May 1854, carried the report of a public meeting at the Town Hall *'for the purpose of taking into consideration the question of market accommodation in the borough'.* The proposal for not only one, but possibly two, covered markets was defeated; the town's corporation could then ill afford such a venture. In the 1830s, the chemist, William Braddock, had promoted such a scheme near the top of Yorkshire Street, but this did not prosper.

Two years after the council had decided against funding its own hall, a private undertaking — the New Market Company — erected a covered market on Curzon Ground; it had cost some £4,000. The private market struggled for nine years before, in 1865, the local authority purchased it for the whimsically exact figure of £10,654 15s.

As the new century beckoned the old building was proving uncomfortable and dangerous, with fragments of glass from the roof bombarding the traders and shoppers below. A 1900 Parliamentary Bill — the Oldham Corporation Act — sanctioned the raising of money for a new bourse, and foundation stones were laid in September 1904. On 6 April 1906, the chairman of the Markets and Baths Committee, Councillor Horrobin, ceremonially unlocked the Henshaw Street doors with a gold key. Further stages of the building were completed during the next two years.

Known as the Victoria Market, though actually erected in Edwardian times, it served the town's buyers and browsers for nearly seventy years before its destruction by fire in the early hours of Saturday 5 October 1974. This conflagration was described at the time as 'the most emotional fire Oldham has known'. Writing in the following Monday's Chronicle, Fred Bottomley probably captured the mood. He likened it to the 'overwhelming sense of shocked grief that friends share at the sudden death of one of their number'.

The following March, beneath a gentle snowfall, the mayor, Ellen Brierley, cut a green ribbon as Oldham's shoppers headed for their replacement 'factory-unit' market hall. It had cost £200,000, and in 1980, following a further £350,000 upgrading, the then mayor, Harold Shanley, formalised the opening, and confirmed the town's new Phoenix as Oldham's 'Elizabethan' market hall.

Curzon Street, c. 1960. A glance along Curzon Street offered this view of the Renaissance gables above the Albion Street entrance to the Victoria Market Hall. Redevelopment has seen the loss of the buildings to the left of the photograph.

Tommyfield, 1920s. In the 1830s the town's governors, the Police Commissioners, decided that Market Place stall-holders would have to trade elsewhere, and for a while they were removed to a pitch near the parish church. Aggrieved at this high-handedness, the traders elected to have their own market, and rented a piece of land known as Curzon Ground, so called because of the landowner, Earl Howe's family name. Formerly, a farmer, Thomas Whittaker, had leased the site and so the market ground became popularly known as Tommyfield.

Mumps, c. 1910. (Photo: courtesy Local Studies Library, Oldham). Wallace's ('Boots and Shoes') traded at Number 30 Mumps, as revealed by Kelly's Directory of 1909. Footwear was also available from Stead & Simpson at Number 34. Boots Cash Chemist dispensed its pills and potions from Number 42. Most celebrated of all the district's emporia was the Mumps bazaar of Buckley & Procter. To reach it — there were departments either side of Lees Road — you would possibly have passed under the railway bridge, a landmark since the Lancashire & Yorkshire Company extended the line to Rochdale in 1863.

Mumps, 1930s. As evidenced by this animated scene, Mumps was clearly a popular and busy shopping area. Place name philologists have suggested that the curious handle derives from 'mumper' (beggar), a workhouse once being situated in the district.

Windsor Road – Bright Street. An evocative vignette of Edwardian street life, with gas light, corner shop, Eton collar and plus-fours. A trade directory of 1905 gives the shop, 34 Windsor Road, as belonging to Oswald Hague, fruiterer. The building has now fallen victim to the demolisher and his bulldozer.

Garden Suburbs, c. 1910. The formal opening of the Garden Suburbs took place on 7 August 1909; it was a Saturday 'favoured by brilliant weather'. The moving spirits of this scheme were the members of the Beautiful Oldham Society.

The early Garden City movement had much impressed these Beautiful Oldhamers, the Letchworth pioneer company's registration dating from 1903. Three years later, a Hampstead Garden Suburb Trust had inspired the local group to similar, with the constituting, in 1906, of the Oldham Garden Suburb Ltd.

A 50-acre site at Hollins was purchased, with plans for a maximum of 14 houses per acre, each dwelling to enjoy its own garden. The first bricks were laid in March 1908, with the earliest occupancy in October. By the day of the ceremony there were already 150 residents. Despite its incomplete state, 'partly-laid roads, bits of bog and water holes', most visitors must have contrasted their 'ordinary cottages and rows of patterned houses' rather unfavourably with the light and airy three bedroom homes on show.

The guest-of-honour was Ebenezer Howard, founder of the Garden City Movement. The great man's peroration offered the prospect of Oldham's transformation to *'a town of beautiful and peaceful homes and dwelling places, a place which they would find refreshing to come to from the outside world, a place of intimate associations, of sound friendships and good memories (Applause).'*

Brompton Street, c. 1907. Immortalising a group of its younger denizens, this study of Brompton Street, situated between Waterloo Street and Park Road, exemplifies Oldham's 'rows of patterned houses'.

Gas lamps were once a feature of almost every street corner. A private enterprise, the Oldham Gas and Water Works Company, was created under Parliamentary authority granted in 1825. Prior to the introduction of gas lighting, illumination relied on oil burners. An Act of 1853 facilitated the transfer of these utilities to the recently incorporated town. The central plant at Greaves Street was accompanied by branches at Royton, Shaw, Leesbrook and Hollinwood; Higginshaw was added later.

By the 1890s electricity was replacing gas at key locations, with carbon arcs at Rhodes Bank, Mumps, Cross Street, Market Place, Curzon Street, King Street and the Town Hall. Tungsten filament lamps supplanted these by 1914 and three years later Yorkshire Street and Union Street were electrically illuminated.

Mumps Station, early 1900s. An Act of 1826 provided for a Manchester & Oldham Railway although these powers were never translated into track and trains. When the first section of the Manchester & Leeds line was opened in July 1839 that inaugural steamer called at Mills Hill, the conductor blasting out 'God Save The Queen' on his bugle.

Werneth Station dates from 1842, linked to Middleton Junction via the 1 in 27 incline. The Lancashire & Yorkshire Railway excavated two tunnels between Werneth and the Clegg Street area opening a new station at Greenacres Moor. This was called Mumps and on 1 November 1847 hundreds of onlookers cheered the maiden departure. Less keen, however, was the public to ride over these fresh rails to Werneth and beyond, *'owing not only to the apprehensions generally felt in passing over a new line, but . . . to the high rate of fares adopted'*.

The Oldham, Ashton & Guide Bridge company (funded partly by the London & Northwestern and Manchester, Sheffield & Lincoln enterprises) provided a station at Clegg Street in 1861, also erecting a 200-yard viaduct at Park Bridge. Passengers were able to journey to Rochdale from Mumps by 2 November 1863.

Until 1880 railway travel to Manchester was through Middleton Junction and its incline. On Whit Monday of that year a half hour service was introduced via Hollinwood.

Central Station was lost (to Doctor Beeching) in the 1960s, with Clegg Street and Glodwick Road already closed to passenger traffic. Mumps, which acquired a new booking-hall in 1956-7, survived Beeching and still serves the town. When the new Mills Hill station was brought into service in 1985, Oldham's railway history had repeated itself (without the bugler's anthem).

The following views, from Tuck's 'Town & City' series, were mailed from Oldham to Suffolk, possibly in 1906–7. The messages are transcribed 'uncensored.'

Hope you will be successful in your Cert. Exam. when the time comes. Did I ever tell you I had a sister a schoolmistress in Oldham? She gets 120 £ yearly. That's good. is it not?
Yrs J. Burrows

Oldham, Top of High Street. 'Many thanks for the beautiful cards to hand. The photograph taken by your brother is very nice indeed. I beg to forward 'Standard' to you — a local newspaper & the 'Conservative' organ. The Liberal weekly is the 'Chronicle' '.

Oldham, Rhodes Bank. *'The street to the right is Yorkshire Street. You can discern the Parish Church in the distance'.*
  Although the tramway standards, decorative lamp and other items of street furniture may have disappeared, much of the view remains recognizable. This area of Oldham was popular with postcard publishers and derives its name from the former Rhodes Estate.

Oldham, The Park Observatory. 'Our local park (Alexandra) is considered a pretty one being about 70 acres in extent. A few years ago a lake for boating was added. There was a lake for the ducks from the commencement.'

The boating lake alluded to was opened in 1903. The Observatory's foundation stone was laid in 1899 as part of the town's Golden Jubilee celebrations.

Many of the illustrations in this album are taken from vintage picture postcards. Perhaps most celebrated of all the Edwardian publishers were the fine art printers, Raphael Tuck & Sons. This firm issued an immense range and number of cards and fanned the early postcard craze with prize competitions; one entrant amassed 20,364 cards, all postally used, in their first competition.

Oldham, Free Library and Art Gallery.   '*As I got these Tuck's cards purposely for you, I'm sending a few. I can let you have some coloured views of Oldham shortly.*'

Described as 'vague Gothic', this testimony to Victorian municipal pride was opened in 1883 for exhibitions, two years later as a reference library and in 1887 for book lending. In former days, 'ladies' could isolate themselves in their own reading room.

Tram Terminus, Hollinwood. A memorial plaque on the wall of Hollinwood's tram building gives the names of the Surveyors and Tramways Committee members and the year, 'A.D. 1910'. Over thirty years before, the Oldham Tramways Order of 1878 permitted the Council to lay tracks and lease them to private operators.

By 1880 the Manchester Carriage and Tramways Company offered a horse-hauled service between Hollinwood and Waterhead. As well as this equine traction, steam trams ('roast potato carts'), under the colours of the Manchester, Bury, Rochdale & Oldham Steam Tramways Co., hissed their way from Royton to Hathershaw via Oldham. The leases of these two enterprises expired in 1901; the year before, Oldham Council had introduced its first electric service.

Parliamentary approval for Oldham to provide its own tram system was won in 1899 and on the Saturday afternoon of 15 December 1900, the Borough's epoch-making electric tram travelled the Middleton Road route from Rochdale Road to the Chadderton boundary.

Electric Tram, High Street. After Oldham's inaugural electric tram was welcomed in 1900 the system became voracious for fresh routes. In 1901 a Lees Road service was introduced, as was one for Hollins and Copster Hill. That year also saw the electrification of a circular Park Road, Glodwick and Cross Street route. In 1902 the Wallshaw Street tramshed was opened with some ceremony; an eight tram convoy took councillors, wives, friends, flags, flowers, bunting and over a ton of foliage to Hollinwood and back to the depot. The Hollinwood–Waterhead service became operational in May 1902. In 1904 the Royton service was extended to Summit and the Shaw Road route continued to Wren's Nest.

Oldham leased track from Crompton, Lees and Royton, and agreements with the transport authorities at Rochdale and Manchester enabled through journeys to these centres by 1907. In 1914 it was possible to reach the dizzy heights of Grains Bar. A direct route to Middleton became available in 1925 following the takeover, from the Middleton Electric Traction Company, of a section of track between Chadderton and Mills Hill.

Oldham's tramway system comprised nearly 20 miles of Corporation owned routes, with almost 6 miles of additional track on lease from neighbouring urban districts.

Motor Bus and Electric Tram, Oldham Town Centre, c. 1940.
Suggestions of a rival to the trams came in 1913 when the town's commuters and shoppers were able to travel by open-top double-decked bus. The first route was from the Town Hall to the Coppice; another trackless service was to Denshaw from Grainsbar. Oldham's initial attempt at motorised omnibus journeying was not a success and these early buses were sold in 1919.

Five years later a motor bus was employed between Hollinwood Station and Mumps via the Coppice, and soon other routes were to appear. By 1928 — the year that tram replacement commenced — Oldham operated 42 buses over 108 miles of road. During the Second World War — the approximate time of this photograph — the ratio of buses to trams was 213 to 27. Oldham's bus garage was built in 1938 on a site area of 180,000 square feet.

Oldham's Last Tram, August 1946. (Photo: courtesy *Oldham Chronicle*). Tramway abandonment had begun in 1928 with the loss of routes from Market Place to Lees and Moorside–Grains Bar. At the end of the Second World War, Oldham's youngest tramcars were over 20 years old, some claiming service prior to the 1914–18 conflict. The last surviving route was the Hollinwood–Waterhead service and the valedictory journey took place on Saturday, 3 August 1946.

The farewell car, illuminated by over 100 lamps and freshly painted in Oldham's white and maroon livery, carried the legends, 'Honourably Retiring' and 'Progressive Efficiency'. The mayor, Alderman Marron, accompanied by the oldest driver and conductor (combined service 80 years) took the 'light princess' over the final circuit, steering the vehicle back to the Wallshaw Street shed for the last time.

Certain of the onlookers improvised their own souvenirs by allowing coins, pins and other objects to be flattened under the wheels. How did the town see this passing of an era? *'Weary, battered, often despised, the trams have been valued public servants and they concluded their labours with the regrets of the sentimental for the old and familiar'*.

All Steamed Up. Not a few local building foundations must have groaned in protest as this leviathan rumbled through the cobbled streets. The Oldham Boiler Works were once situated at the top of Henshaw Street whilst Lees & Wrigley's Greenbank Mills, for whom the monstrous cylinder is destined, spun their yarns at the junction of Greengate Street and Glodwick Road. Both have now gone, the former long since, but in Oldham's 1949 centenary souvenir, Lees & Wrigley's were still advertising as 'Cotton Spinners and Doublers of Fine and Medium Combed Yarns'.

Waterloo School, Hardy Street. At a special meeting of the Oldham Town Council, convened for 7 December 1870, it was agreed, *'That application be made to the Education Department under Section 12 of the Elementary Education Act, 1870, for the formation of a School Board for the district of the Borough of Oldham'.* Forster's Elementary Education Act was a major milestone in the history of public sector schooling. At first, elementary education was neither free nor compulsory under the Act, although local boards were able to enact by-laws to enforce attendance. School boards were elected directly, and in that sense, independent of the local authority, although they were empowered to precept a rate through the council.

Oldham's inaugural board met on 19 January 1871, with the Reverend R.M. Davies as chairman. The first schools erected by the board at Westwood and Smith Street were opened on 21 July 1873. Before this, premises has been rented from organisations such as the Ragged Schools Society.

New Schools were built as the years rolled by: Hathershaw (1878), Wellington Street (1879), Roundthorn (1881), Waterhead (1883), Watersheddings (1884), Scottfield and Beever Street (1885). In the 1890s the board acquired schools at Werneth and Derker, and in 1893 moved into its new offices in Union Street West. A school medical officer was appointed in 1880, about the same time that the establishments were staffed with drill instructors (in 1887, 1384 pairs of dumb-bells were purchased!)

Waterloo School, photographed here before the First World War, admitted its first pupils in 1887, and served its latter days as a secondary modern institute before closure in 1962. Prior to demolition it functioned as a police attendance centre and youth club. In the early years Waterloo was known as a higher grade school. It provided science laboratories and offered French and Latin studies. After the turn of the century the buildings housed a secondary school before its transfer to Greengate Street, eventually becoming Greenhill Grammar School.

Hollinwood Council School Football Team, 1923. On 1 January 1904, the Oldham School Board disappeared and was replaced by the town's Education Committee. The former board schools became council schools, as the new local education authority assumed its pedagogic role.

Hollinwood opened its doors on 9 February 1903 as a board school, and bade its farewell in 1966, after merging with Greenhill Grammar to create the Kaskenmoor School on Roman Road.

Writing in 1966 of his childhood recollections at the school during the 1908 to 1913 period, a former Hollinwood pupil recounts the remarkable success on the football field. After winning the Oldham Schools' League Championship for the twelfth time, the shield was presented to the school and hung in the lower hall. They played their home games on a ground behind Chapel Road, and cotton workers, after clocking off on Saturday morning, lined the pitch two and three deep. There was even a rousing refrain.

> 'Play up, Freehold', you'd hear the captain cry,
> 'Heads down, you'll never get o'er the rye.
> Your colours are blue and white,
> You try with all your might
> But you can't beat the boys from Hollinwood.'

Boundary Park Football Ground. This rare action photograph was taken sometime before the First World War, although exact date and match details are not available. Note the observation gallery on top of the then main stand; the present structure was erected about 1913.

The Boundary Park arena was laid out and enclosed for the Oldham County Football Club. The first sod was turned in July 1896, following a brass-band-led march from the Willow Bank Hotel on Featherstall Road. Soccer's kick-off at Sheepfoot Lane was made by the M.P., Robert Ascroft, at a friendly encounter with Chorley on 19 September of that year. The weather though, less than amiable, drove the local parliamentarian to the shelter of the dressing rooms, and caused the game's abandonment.

Following Oldham County's collapse, the new Oldham Athletic took residence at Sheepfoot Lane in 1899, but were forced to move to another home, Hudson Fold, owing to a tenancy dispute during the 1900–1 season. They remained at Hudson Fold until 1906 when they negotiated a new lease and returned to Boundary Park, where they have been ensconced ever since.

OLDHAM ATHLETIC.

Hanson (*Trainer*)   Hodson   Fay   Shovelbottom   Hewitson   Hamilton   Kelly   Mr. Ashworth (*Sec.*)
Newton   Hesham   Dodds   Walders   Hancock   Wilson   Swarbrick

Oldham Athletic, 1907–8. Organised football was a product of the nineteenth-century public schools. They adopted the people's mob games and codified them to suit their own playing needs. Each school played under its own rules, and as a means of imposing a measure of uniformity, several ex-university and school players met in London in 1863 to create a regulating body; it was called the Football Association. The 'Muscular Christian' missionaries of legend then took the sport to the industrial centres of the north and midlands. By the 1880s the champions were no longer called Oxford University and Old Etonians; the titans came from West Bromwich and Aston, Blackburn and Preston. Professionalism was sanctioned in 1885 and in order to provide regular fixtures (and hence income) a Football League was first contested in the 1888–9 season.

Although several Lancashire teams were founder members of the Football League, there was no Oldham representative until 1907. The town had opted for the oval-ball game and scrimmages, so that when Oldham County entertained an Everton eleven fielding three internationals in a match staged in September 1895, two-thirds of the onlookers were reported as being quite bewildered by the spectacle. The players changed, much to the discomfort of the Merseyside aristocrats, at the Featherstall and Junction Inn, the game being played on a ground near the Pine Mill. County headed not for soccer glory, alas, but to the bankruptcy courts.

Football's fortunes were revived in 1899 when a local amateur club, Pine Villa, adopted the name, Oldham Athletic, and gained admittance to the Manchester Alliance. By 1904 they had been elected to the Lancashire Combination. The club registered as a limited liability company in May 1906, and applied to the Football League, failing by one vote. At the end of the 1906–7 semester the players toured the town in a convoy of wagonettes; they were champions of the Combination and holders of the Lancashire Alliance Cup, and the band struck up 'See the Conquering Hero Comes'. Again they solicited the League for membership, and once more rejection came their way: the management suspected a Midlands conspiracy against the Red Rose. In desperation they applied to the Southern League, then a powerful competition, but the votes went to Bradford. Finally, Oldham Athletic were invited to play with football's elite on the resignation, due to financial problems, of Burslem.

Athletic's league baptism was at Stoke on 7 September 1907. The Chronicle's man-at-the-match reported a 3–1 Oldham victory and the paper styled the portentous event, 'Potters Potted.'

Sincerely yours,
H. Matthews
(Oldham Athletic) Sept 23-9-11

T. Ashton.   M. Lawton.   J. E. Lees.   J. A. Mellodew.   H. Hoyle.   Wm. Ward *(Pro.)*
H. Sutcliffe.   S. Haggas.   T. Mellodew.   W. Mellodew.   S. Pogson.

Moorside Cricket Team, 1906.   The Central Lancashire League was first contested during the 1892 cricket season; Oldham and Royton were founder members. Further local interest was aroused with the subsequent admission to the combination of Werneth and Crompton.

During the early part of the present century, the clubs of the C.L.L. also welcomed these flannelled battlers from the lofty altitude of Moorside. The mill-owning family of Mellodew provided three-elevenths of the 1906 campaigners. The captain, Tom, and his brothers, William and James, were described as the 'backbone' of the side.

Herbert Sutcliffe not only shared his name with the famed Yorkshire hero, but also celebrated the same birthday, and when not at the crease, worked at the Cairo Mill. William Mellodew and Mitchell Lawton once made a record-breaking first-wicket stand of 262 against Crompton. William Ward, the season's professional, played several years for Warwickshire and was accorded the epithet, 'a bit of a lad'.

If 1906 was not their finest season, the following year they entered the record books as champions of the C.L.L.

Howard Matthews, Goalkeeper, Oldham Athletic.   The Latics won promotion to the First Division in 1910. Success was only secured in the last match of the season, defeating rivals Hull City, before a crowd of over 29,000 at Boundary Park.

The period 1910 to 1915 had the team competing on equal terms with the giants of football. In 1913 an FA Cup semi-final was lost by one goal, and the 1915 League Championship saw them runners-up to Everton.

Men such as Fay and Roberts were not only talented footballers, but campaigned for players' rights through their trade union. George Woodger represented England, and Howard Matthews, whose signed portrait is reproduced here, served as Oldham's custodian before the First World War and into the 1920s.

Entrance, Alexandra Park. Alexandra Park was opened by the mayor, Josiah Radcliffe, on 28 August 1865; it was the first day of Oldham Wakes and the rain was unrelenting.

The American Civil War had caused such a shortage of raw cotton, and consequent unemployment, that Oldham's Poor Law Guardians assisted over 28,000 people in 1862, and the following year, one in five of the population was destitute.

Through its Public Works (Manufacturing Districts) Act, the Government advanced loans at advantageous rates of interest to encourage work-creating projects. Oldham resolved to lay out a public park, purchasing 72 acres of land at Swine Clough. In December 1863, the mayor, John Riley, turned the first sod.

On the day of the ceremonial, such was the downpour, that a grand procession planned for the celebration, was delayed and shortened. Despite the inhospitable elements, a crowd of 1,300 souls assembled at the park square to see the mayor make his formal entrance after unlocking the gates with a gilded key. Proceeding to the old refreshment room, the congregation heard the park's history delivered by the Town Clerk; speeches were made by sundry worthies, and the Old Hundredth sung by those with lungs to do so. Before departing for the Town Hall feast and more speeches, a selection of mementos — including coins and newspapers — was deposited in a cavity of the corner-stone at the park's entrance.

One of the local M.P.s, Mr Platt, opined that '... *the noblest bequest that had ever been given to Oldham ... had been opened that day*'.

Refreshment Rooms, Alexandra Park. Before its demolition in 1970, those who cared to glance to the higher facade of this solid pavilion, could read the date of the park's opening carved into the masonry. Plans had envisaged a museum for the upper floor and several exhibits had been contributed by the day of the inaugural ceremony. It also contained a pair of allegorical stained glass windows.

The refreshment room was an original feature of Alexandra Park, named in honour of the Prince of Wales' Danish bride, as were the Italianate entrance building and a band shelter, known familiarly as the 'Lions' Den'. The duck pond, too, dates from 1865, although the boating lake came later. Of the statuary, 'Blind Joe' was unveiled in 1868, 'Rebecca at the Well' suffered vandalism in 1956, and Ascroft's likeness was presented in 1903. John Platt once surveyed the Town Hall from his granite pedestal before migration to the top walk. The 'Boy and Dolphin' fountain was donated by Josiah Radcliffe. The Pagoda's foundation stone was laid on 17 June 1899, the day of the town's golden jubilee festivities.

In 1975, when the park was 110 years old and showing its wrinkles, initiatives were taken jointly by Oldham and the Greater Manchester Council to have the ageing monument designated a conservation area. This protection was also afforded to the neighbouring Alexandra and Queen's Roads, which were developed in the nineteenth century to help defray the park's costs.

Robert Ascroft Statue, Unveiling Ceremony 1903. (Photo: courtesy Local Studies Library, Oldham). The 'Workers' Friend' sat as Tory M.P. for Oldham from 1895 until his death in 1899. Ascroft was solicitor to the local Cotton Operatives' Trade Union, and so it was fitting that the secretary of this association should unveil the memorial in Alexandra Park.

Winston Churchill, in his autobiography, *My Early Life : 1874–1908,* relates how, in 1899, the Oldham M.P. had suggested that Churchill run alongside him in the next election, as the other member for Oldham, J.F. Oswald, was in poor health. History tells us that it was Ascroft who passed on, forcing a by-election. Oswald resigned and the two new Conservative candidates, Churchill and Mawdsley, were beaten by the Liberals, Emmott and Runciman.

Churchill, who was, however, elected M.P. for the Borough in 1900, wrote *'Robert Ascroft was greatly respected by the Oldham working folk. They made a subscription of more than £2,000, the bulk collected in very small sums, to set up a statue . . . They stipulated . . . that the money was not to go to anything useful; no extensions to a Library, no fountain even, just a memorial. They did not want, they said, to give a present to themselves.'*

Lakeside Promenade, Alexandra Park. Picture postcard published by Abel Heywood & Son of Oldham, who once traded from the Citadel Buildings on Union Street. This card was despatched from Hollinwood to Newcastle-on-Tyne and carries the cancellation for August 1911.

'Tower Bridge', Alexandra Park Gates. The 1953 Coronation inspired this incongruous transfer from London to Lancashire. Photograph *c.* 1960.

Opening of the Boating Lake, Alexandra Park. (Photo: courtesy Local Studies Library, Oldham). At the turn-of-the-century, the Oldham Park Committee obtained borrowing power of £12,000 for constructing a boating lake. In 1983 the Council voted to spend £380,000 on relining the lake bed in an attempt to remedy serious leakage problems, and a further £20,000 on improving the lakeside's appearance.

The original idea of using the valley between Kings Road and Alexandra Park for a boating lake was put to the local authority by a group of businessmen. The site was declared to be an eyesore and a public nuisance — it had once been a rubbish tip. These entrepreneurs offered to construct the amenity in exchange for a period of rent free operation; it would then become the town's absolute property. The reply came thus, '. . . why cannot we make the lake ourselves and let the ratepayers enjoy any pecuniary advantage which may accrue.'

The first bag of cement for the bed was duly emptied on 28 May 1902, exactly one year to the day before the official dedication and opening. There was a boathouse/refreshment room (teetotallers only) and three islands ('miniature castellated turrets'). The new mere had a water surface area of 5 acres with a depth for boating of 3½ feet. In winter this was reduced to 2 feet so that 'without fear or trembling the fascinating and invigorating pastime of skating can be indulged in'. Electric illuminations from the islands, landing-stage and boathouse offered nocturnal sculling. The lake was equipped with an electric launch, *The Mayoress* (1d per passenger once round the lake), and 36 rowing boats, named after the wives and daughters of the Park Committee. The first manager was 'Admiral' Sam Axon, assisted by two men and a 'youth'; each willing

'. . . to devote a few minutes' attention to teaching timid youths or maidens the art of rowing and managing a skiff or a canoe'.

The grand day of the launchings was 'favoured with propitious weather'. There was bunting from boathouse to flagstaff; palms and indiarubber plants decorated the platform. To allay the fears of the tremulous, the Council's guests included a Mr Cook of Preston, who was the reputed saviour of thirty-five lives in the Ribble. The railways sounded a *feu de joie* of detonators as an engine ran over several fog-signals, and victory in the councillors' boat race went to Messrs Hodges and Sixsmith, with one luckless burgher steering his craft into an island.

Grand Theatre, King Street, c. 1910. This prospect, on the corner of Union Street and King Street, was once dominated by the austere bulk of Sinkinson's Mill. On Christmas Eve 1908, the curtain of the town's new Grand Theatre and Opera House rose for the first time. Those Yuletide Oldhamers were enchanted by the pantomime magic of *Aladdin*. Its boards later offered Gothic drama and high opera, but by the 1930s live theatre was under attack from the growing popularity of film. Oldham's variety theatre, the Palace, became the Odeon cinema, and the Grand was henceforth known as the Gaumont.

The Gaumont cinema opened on 14 June 1937, with a screening of *My Man Godfrey,* featuring Carol Lombard and William Powell. The guest of honour at this gala baptism was George Formby, who was not allowed to depart without singing a ukelele-accompanied ditty or two.

After the war the town acquired one of its most familiar (and functional) landmarks when, in 1947, the Finance Committee was advised that arrangements had been made to place a public clock above the building.

Just as greasepaint had given way to cinema, so by the early 1960s television had affected cinematic entertainment. The Gaumont became a ten-pin bowling alley and ballroom, the Astoria. Of one memorable evening in February 1963, the *Oldham Chronicle* reported, '*Nearly 2,000 teenagers stormed Oldham's Astoria Ballroom . . . to see the current top rock group, The Beatles*'.

Top Rank sold out to a north-east enterprise, the Bailey Organisation, so that by 1973 the old Grand was tempting fun people to disco-cabaret and go-go girls. Later came Romeo's and Juliet's, then in 1985, its transmutation produced Butterfly's and Over the Rainbow (fun drinkery).

Shaw Prize Brass Band, 1909. By Edwardian times there must have been brass bands at almost every turn. Oldham and its surrounding districts had outfits at Glodwick, Lees, Delph, Dobcross, Diggle and Waterhead. There were bands sacred and profane — Salvation Army, missions and public houses. The Park and Cemeteries Committee agreed to pay £3 per ensemble for the 1906 Summer season in Alexandra Park; Brown's Military Band offered their marches and melodies gratis in aid of the Oldham Poor Children's Holiday Fund.

It was the Shaw Prize Band, though, which returned home early one September Sunday morning in 1909 as 'Champions of Great Britain and Colonies'. The National Championships at the Crystal Palace in south London, held on Saturday 25 September, had witnessed the Cromptonians' all-conquering success, with their 'brilliant rendering' of the test-piece — selections from Wagner's *Flying Dutchman*.

Until this triumph, the 1909 competition season had proved a poor one, the journey to Sydenham having to be funded from the harvest of a whip-round.

Despite these earlier tribulations, the leader, Mr Rimmer, batoned his musicians into concert pitch for the challenge and his men's lungs did not falter. Such was the low expectation of success that no pre-arranged victory celebrations greeted the bandsmen on their homecoming, but the following Tuesday, the heroes were fêted by 10,000 well-wishers at the Town Hall, and on the market ground, 30,000 people gathered 'frantic with delight'. The scenes were, according to the *Oldham Chronicle's* man at the revelry, 'unparalleled in the history of Crompton'.

Oldham PSA Orchestra. The PSA or Pleasant Sunday Afternoon movement began in West Bromwich, quickly spreading to other industrial and heavily populated areas. It was an attempt by Nonconformist churches to bring Sunday School ideas to adults. Meetings included Bible readings, hymns, prayers and 'uplifting songs'; its motto was 'Brief, Bright and Brotherly'.

In Oldham, the local branch celebrated its golden jubilee in 1942 and boasted that 2,000 total abstinence pledges had been signed.

Described as non-sectarian and non-political, the brotherhood was introduced to the town at the Waterloo Street Trinity Wesleyan Church. The first president, Mr J.W. Dent, was a schoolmaster and preacher. During the first year a Labour Bureau was opened to relieve the effects of widespread unemployment. Services held in the King Street Co-operative Hall and Empire Theatre attracted congregations of over 2,000.

Bowling greens and tennis courts at Fitton Hill were owned by the PSA, and musical concerts, as typified by this photograph of the orchestra in Alexandra Park, were given and said to have been 'greatly appreciated'. A newspaper — *The Oldham PSA Leader* — appeared in June 1903.

Oldham Concertina Band, 1908. Oldham's squeeze-box victors pose for their team photograph, with pride of place given to the shield won at the Crystal Palace Band Festival. In 1908 the event was contested on 26 September, with the test-piece — 'Sunshine and Shade' — performed under the guidance of the conductor/bandmaster, Mr J.A. Astley.

This photographic postcard was mailed on 30 September and carries the message of success (as well as the whereabouts of Joe's hamper). *'Dear Joe, Your hamper is at Bewdley station. The Saturday after we come back Joe we got second prize at Belle Vue. We got the first prize at Crystal Palace London last Saturday. This sheild [sic] on this post card we have won it 2 year running. Hoping it will find you all well from your affectionate friend John.'*

Union Street, c. 1910. In the 1850s the editor of Edwin Butterworth's history of Oldham wrote of Union Street that '... *it bids fair to be, at no distant day, not only the principal street in the town, but in point of architectural adornment to surpass places of more pretension than Oldham has been hitherto considered*'.

When this photograph was taken, the street was indeed the town's grandest thoroughfare. The Lyceum (1856), Library (1883), public baths (1854) and Salvation Army Citadel (1886) gave it a notable architectural profile.

In the distance, this scene reveals the location of the future Grosvenor cinema on the corner of Peter Street to be a plot of land surrounded by hoardings.

The ornamental tramway standards appeared in the town's highways as electrification proceeded from 1900. Decorative they were, but not to everyone's satisfaction: the Watch Committee was advised in May 1902, of the '*difficulty that had arisen in the control of vehicular traffic in streets where tram car poles had been set up in the middle of the thoroughfare*'.

These 'tram car poles' have now gone, of course, as have other landmarks. The French pavilion frontage of the old baths (erected as a memorial to Sir Robert Peel) has been replaced by dazzling red-brick offices. The Saint Peter's school (*c.* 1835) is lost, as is the street's Methodist church, which, however, retains its partial façade in the Brunswick Square scheme. The Citadel was demolished in the late 1960s to make way for Phoenix House.

Union Street, 1920s. Union Street was Oldham's own celluloid highway. In June 1937 the street hosted a typical pantheon of cinematic heroes and heroines: Mae West (Grosvenor), George Robey (Victory), Carol Lombard and William Powell (Gaumont), Freddie Bartholomew (Odeon) and Joan Crawford and Robert Taylor (Palladium).

This photograph suggests what a fine building the Grosvenor cinema was in its prime. Before demolition in 1985, the town knew the venue as Bo-Bo's nightspot. In August 1920 this new baroque 'Super Kinema' was enthusiastically described as ' . . . *the acme of perfection so far as picture theatre has gone in conception, commodiousness and comfort . . .*'

The Palladium opened as a cinema in 1913, whilst the Victory started life as a theatre, known variously as the Adelphi, Gaiety and Hippodrome, before conversion to the movies in 1920.

The Odeon, originally the Palace Theatre (1908), became a cinema in the mid-thirties. In 1976 it was converted to a three-in-one, Rank Leisure closing the loss-maker seven years later.

The castellated fortress to the right of the view was the Salvation Army headquarters, now the site of Phoenix House.

Waterhead. The village of Waterhead is known to many as a bus or (at the time of this photograph) tram terminus. Even before the horse trams reached its boundary, stage coaches on the Oldham–Huddersfield turnpike road rested here.

An ecclesiastical parish was formed in 1843; the first vicar, the Reverend Patrick Reynolds, began a building fund that saw its fruition in Holy Trinity Church, erected in 1847. Mutual improvement was fostered through societies such as the Waterhead Educational Institution and Waterhead People's College.

After Oldham won its Charter of Incorporation, the local municipal ward was known as Waterhead Mill, reflecting the vital rôle of the textile industry in the district's life; indeed Edwin Butterworth's history identifies several eighteenth-century manufacturers, at that time engaged more in the woollen than cotton trade.

One Jacob Tweedale, whose father came with Prince Charlie in 1745, lived in a thatched cottage at Waterhead, and sired a line that included the former mayors of Oldham, Frank and Arnold Tweedale.